CU00841177

Copyright © 2012 by Criss Jami

Published in the United States by Criss Jami
ISBN 1-9836-8895-9

Venus In Arms

A poetry book by Criss Jami

1) This Is Sisyphus
2) Ink (A Storm In My Soul)
3) Omnia Causa Fiunt
4) A Wry Face
5) Aesthetically Appealing
6) Stylus (Of The Wildest Dreams)
7) Stuck In Traffic
8) To Spring In Summer And Fall By Winter
9) Éminence Grise (Won't You Teach Me)
10) ...For The Forgotten
11) Mea Maxima Culpa, Cybernational Coma
12) Sense To Survive
13) Kiss The Blarney Stone
14) Metal
15) Film Noir (Trade Some Resistance)
16) Slipshod Lover
17) The Order Of Mistakes
18) Pressure Of The Hellhounds
19) My Marionette
20) Haze
21) Münchausen
22) Fable
23) Countdown To Kill Me
24) Lovecraft Theme
25) Wahrheit For My Sycophant (My Psychopath)
26) Shatter Me Sinfonia
27) Center Of War
28) Jump The Gun
29) For Veritas Aequitas
30) Like St. Raphael

I would rather be an artist than a leader. Ironically, a leader has to follow the rules.

This Is Sisyphus

Over time
I taught me how to outdo myself
After awhile
Darling it shocked too loud now I tune out the world

If this is Sisyphus yes I'm in love with this
And if I regretted the jokes I've thrown
Well I'd be more alone than you know
'Cause this is what I do
Baby I send kisses just for you
But it's up to you whether or not this love is true

So what's a legible heart
In a clever devil of God
Who just missed the mark

Yes I wish I knew, my friend
But I can't comprehend what doesn't end

No we won't trick the treat, make your heart skip a beat
That is unless you want me
So what's your pleasure it's whatever you please
But if I started to like you I wouldn't let you see
Baby that'd set me free

Oh what's a legible heart
In a clever devil of God
Who just missed the mark

Yes I wish I knew, my friend
But I can't comprehend what doesn't end
I can't comprehend what doesn't end

To say that one waits a lifetime for his soulmate to come around is a paradox. People eventually get sick of waiting, take a chance on someone, and by the art of commitment become soulmates, which takes a lifetime to perfect.

Ink (A Storm In My Soul)

Il tempo è burrascoso
Because your temper creates a storm in my soul
A storm in my soul

So which of us pulled away
And made a fool of a little bit of everything
Oh you say it's high time I forgot how to play games

Like I'm holding a controller solely to control her

I didn't flip the switch nor did I turn it off
A ridiculous decision girl it's still my loss
And by the minute we'll feel the frost
Of Boreas and it's
It's right when I swore we had it all

So we're pros at a love that we fail to practice
A business
One where we sell the madness
It's not some fatal happiness
It's backwards
A game over and a railway to has-been

Like I'm holding a controller coldly to control her

I didn't flip the switch nor did I turn it off
A ridiculous decision girl it's still my loss
And by the minute we'll feel the frost
Of Boreas and it's
It's right, you're bored if we have it all

So I've written too much to speak a word worth saying
I'll just let the ink slide like my fingers are praying
I'm adjusting to a lot of things lately
Surely you understand what these inklings are making

Like I'm holding a controller only to control her

An over-indulgence of anything, even something as pure as water, can intoxicate.

Omnia Causa Fiunt

Omnia causa fiunt
But I'm wondering why we cease to look, for what we really want
Divide et impera
But I see it getting better, I see it getting better

I never really saw the celerity of your heart
When busy fighting off the Kierkegaardian part
I listened to Plutarch
As you threw out something of ours
Like humans are shoes you only use certain hours

This love is technology I refuse to understand
A runway too small for my plane to land
How is it that I always get the upper hand
Baby don't ask me if you won't take my hand
Oh no I wouldn't harass you
But in a way
I'd break your chance

'Cause you want a man from Venus
Who stands for love and your vengeful genius
A reflection of who you are
Oh yes it's who you are

Was it trying too hard or a little too little
That time we met up yes we parted a few rivers
That's the power of the way that we're living
Say it's the sour taste of our bittersweet division

This love is technology I refuse to understand
A runway too small for my plane to land
Oh love is technology I refuse to understand
Yes a runway too small for my plane to land

"We ought not to treat living creatures like shoes or household belongings, which when worn with use we throw away." ~Plutarch

A Wry Face

My sense of coherence is a riddling talk
Like I don't know the difference or it's nothing at all
Let's prepare us for the trickiness
And baby spare us what's missing 'cause
I swear I need a break from this love it's now killing us

You are right because you are wry
It's you and I and your crooked eyes
A life at the asylum baby my mansion in disguise

You are right because you are wry
I'll forever like your eyes
A life at the asylum say it's a mansion in disguise

Anger's like a battery that leaks acid right out of me
And it starts from the heart 'til it reaches my outer me
But you're a lover not a fighter
You lit love without a lighter
Let's prepare us for this trickiness
'Cause I swear I'm rising higher

You are right because you are wry
It's you and I and your crooked eyes
A life at the asylum baby my mansion in disguise

You are right because you are wry
I'll forever like your eyes
A life at the asylum say it's a mansion in disguise

"To crooked eyes truth may wear a wry face." ~J.R.R.
Tolkien (Gandalf)

Aesthetically Appealing

Tell me to sing you a song and darling I'll build a guitar for you
We'll play the gardens, for kings and gods, that's simply the card
you choose

You see I'll never be exactly what you want me to be
Because I dream of what seems to be a harder creed
Aesthetically appealing, in the mind it always will be
But as for the journey yes it's learning to deal with the suffering

And of all the minds in my mind
They all advise me to hide inside a little something I can't deny
Oh legend of the times
Oh heart that never dies

Because our heroes are alive and well
Through a mastermind who could smile through Hell
Our heroes are alive and well
Through a mastermind who could smile through Hell

Yes it's true
I'm the biggest fool on the planet
But I'd be a fool to wanna change it
I'm a lion in a strange land
Untamed baby I'm deranged and
I attack the made man

And of all the minds in my mind
They all advise me to hide inside a little something I can't deny
Oh legend of the times
Oh heart that never dies

Because our heroes are alive and well
Through a mastermind who could smile through Hell
Our heroes are alive and well
Through a mastermind who could smile through Hell

True rebels hate their own rebellion. They know by experience that it is not a cool and glamorous lifestyle; it takes a courageous fool to say things that have not been said and to do things that have not been done.

Stylus (Of The Wildest Dreams)

She didn't wear rings, a girl of simplicity
Genius, said hard things in the simplest way
Yes a fool in the heart of the city I stay

With wires weak to the hub
In dire need of a drug
The kind that fries
Away the mind
When you see the wise is nothing but love

I forgot what happened
Though I know it's still lasting
Just ask her, from the world said she's fasting
To turn back with the heart of her master

Stylus
Of the wildest dreams
And they're never as crazy as they seem
Dances
A fire in my eyes and it's
It's raging for you and me

He always liked a girl, a man of many worlds
Foolish, say and complicate the hardest way
A genius to the heart of Venus he was born astray

With wires weak to the hub
In dire need of a drug
The kind that fries
Away the mind
When you see the wise is nothing but love

I forgot what happened
Though I know it's still lasting
Just ask him, from the world said he's fasting
To turn back with the heart of his master

Stylus
Of the wildest dreams
And they're never as crazy as they seem
Dances
A fire in my eyes and it's
It's raging for you and me

And the smallest looks are the most crucial ones
Like a virus contagious
Eros on the hunt
The smallest looks, the crucial ones
Outrageous, outrageous
Eros with a gun

Stylus
Oh the wildest dreams
And they're never as crazy as they seem
Dances
A fire in my eyes darling
It's raging for you and me

Confidence is like a dragon where, for every head cut off, two more heads grow back.

Stuck In Traffic

I won't be stuck in traffic 'til I see how rugged my path is
And right now I'm loving how fast my troubles are fasting

No they don't bother me oh realizing I'm psychopathic
A wild beast, baby I'm gladly running after
Yes a thing called peace outlasting any madness

The devil fears me oh he's feeling
Like a fragment of a fraction
No he won't come near me
'Cause his hat trick's out of practice

I'm a fool because I'm faithful
A fool because I'm faithful

If you're doubted darling that's how it happens
You go through things that're bound to batter
Before the golden garden or cyan city
Oh you see everything baby prior to peace

I'm a fool because I'm faithful
A fool because I'm faithful

In order to share one's true brilliance one initially has to risk looking like a fool: genius is like a wheel that spins so fast, it at first glance appears to be sitting still.

To Spring In Summer And Fall By Winter

Every season there's a reason it's
The construction of a winner
In the spring, next spring
Baby reborn sinners

It hurts to see you hurt
And the night we were on the monorail it worked
Is this for you or me
And you signaled I'll know when I start listening

To see the ends of the earth
To speak Venerean words
You favored my patience
Though I still hated waiting

And since you're mute
Yes I'll say it for you

Silver bullets and a stake in the heart
But the cross still awakens my heart
I'm the freak of nature that's all
Darling it's not the way that you are

The spring comes and maybe ('til then)
Your asylum is what makes me (win)
To spring in summer and fall by winter

Oh the spring comes baby
Your asylum is what makes me
To spring in summer and fall by winter

You stitched open the eyes and
Left a few
I used on the mouth
To spite you
It's how I know that

I want you
So again I'll show that
I love you

Silver bullets and a stake in the heart
But the cross still awakens my heart
I'm the freak of nature that's all
Darling it's not the way that you are

The spring comes and maybe ('til then)
Your asylum is what makes me (win)
To spring in summer and fall by winter

Oh the spring comes baby
Your asylum is what makes me
To spring in summer and fall by winter

Spring in summer and fall by winter
Spring in summer and fall by winter
Spring in summer and fall by winter
We spring in summer and fall by winter
And the spring, reborn sinners

Faithfulness imparts God's reason for all circumstances. No matter what the world says, losing is no longer an option.

Éminence Grise (Won't You Teach Me)

He met you on a Sunday
Last week (last week)
In a jacket that hugs itself (and the knees grew weak)
Éminence grise, éminence grise

Hit rock bottom he said it's what he did
Like a child of Sodom and inside a kid
Pressure, pressure
And standards, the guilt of the aged
Well-mannered but filling a cage

Éminence grise, éminence grise
Right there and insane baby we look too far
Éminence grise
Won't you teach me so close but no cigar

Pont de Normandie crumbles
In his mind as you
You watch him tumble
And tried to speak, by the tongue he fumbled
"While you're here darling watch me stumble"
As I

Walk and love
We're walking in love
For the walk of love

Éminence grise, éminence grise
Right there and insane baby we look too far
Éminence grise
Won't you teach me so close but no cigar

The Proverbs you sing colors
The image of you, paint me
Not the council, not the judge
Like pools of mud

Like fools for blood who say what's free
As we

Walk and love
We're walking in love
At the touch of love

Éminence grise, éminence grise
Right there and insane baby we look too far
Éminence grise
Won't you teach me so close but no cigar

And you say to
Walk and love
We're walking in love
To the test of love

There is a master way with words which is not learned but is instead developed: a deaf man develops exceptional vision, a blind man exceptional hearing, a silent man, when given a piece of paper…

...For The Forgotten

He feels he's missing something
Trying to build with the minutes dropping
Will you give him something
That you have
He's gone mad

They try to help him out of this
Hit or miss the only trick
To success, his mistress of illness
Can you help him out
He says "stop and get out"

She learns the trivial way
The way the mind deteriorates
A life of doubt and where is the world
Does it care for the girl

They'll cast judgment 'til the day she's dead
Like she needs another voice in the head
She expected more advice, I said
Not a word... I listened... something she never had

You're a gift
To an earth you feel you don't belong
And to give your all for a piece torn off
With a thorn in the hip and more pissed off
But remember, the devil's happy when the critics run you off

In an extroverted society, the difference between an introvert and an extrovert is that an introvert is often unconsciously deemed guilty until proven innocent.

Mea Maxima Culpa, Cybernational Coma

Always and never
Always and never heard it before
Forever and ever

Is it now you have the glamorous low-life
The hidden scum inside
You have it won't you share with her
Free the bluebird inside

Mechanical greenery nurtures the earth
But you want the love, just her

Is it faith in the sound of logic
To say "a fool's life is a dream"
We're savvy tools of reality
Angeldæmon come to me

Mea culpa, mea culpa, mea maxima culpa
Mea culpa, mea culpa, mea maxima culpa
This is for the cybernational coma

Why the vegan life to get through the night I
I know you've already died
You have a little to share with her
But you're holding onto dimes

Tyrannical girl will nurture your earth
The love is absurd like my heretical church

Is it faith in the sound of logic
To say "a fool's life is a dream"
We're savvy tools of reality
Angeldæmon come to me

Mea culpa, mea culpa, mea maxima culpa
Mea culpa, mea culpa, mea maxima culpa

This is for the cybernational coma

Let it be known
Oh beautiful scum of the nightglow town
Let it be known spread life around
Let it be known
Oh beautiful scum of the nightglow town
Let it be known spread life around

In the age of technology there is constant access to vast amounts of information. The basket overflows; people get overwhelmed; the eye of the storm is not so much what goes on in the world, it is the confusion of how to think, feel, digest, and react to what goes on.

Sense To Survive

We had the sense to survive
But since December died
We forgot what was life so
No I'm not
Living a lie at the least
No I won't
Trust your word to me

If I know my heart hardens
Then there's a soul left to lose
The compass rose turns
As the greenery blues
It's a storm in a screen that I'm looking through
To look at you
And we call it cyber-fighting
Like that's the good news

How did it get there
And what did it cost
That I don't really care
I don't count a loss
I just know what I want
And it can't be touched
And it can't be seen
You see my instincts shoot open the richie rich scene

We had the sense to survive
But since December died
We forgot what was life so
No I'm not
Living a lie at the least
No I won't
Trust your word to me

Don't excuse it Ms.
Oh it's something I've noticed

And I see that it's
It's proudly displayed in your flower bouquet it's
A name erased though you embrace the praise

We had the sense to survive
But since December died
We forgot what was life so
No I'm not
Living a lie at the least
No I won't
Trust your word to me

I just know what I want
And it can't be touched
And it can't be seen
You see my instincts shoot open the richie rich scene
It's a heart that doesn't change over the next big thing
A heart that doesn't change oh for the next big thing

If the entire world sought to make itself worthy of happiness rather than make itself happy, then the entire world would be happy.

Kiss The Blarney Stone

My time is ticking, dividing pretty little things
To count them one by one
To kiss the Blarney Stone, it's already shown
That your mouth is a loaded gun

But let's not bow to a déjà vu ending
It's something I don't really find too friendly
I have so many vices
And all so pretentious
I can read a liar
And still like their kisses

I found you with a Stella Artois
Empty and far, far gone
Many miles apart and lost
You're my libertine, a heart without a cause

And my time is ticking, dividing pretty little things
To count them one by one
To kiss the Blarney Stone, it's already shown
That your mouth is a loaded gun

But let's not grow with our roots in the ground
I'm a traveler, a loner that's been around
Baby to seek is not a crisis
But worse it's
Like a cigarette to the eyelids
But worth it
And you can't really hide it
Oh girl 'cause

I found you with a Stella Artois
Empty and far, far gone
Many miles apart and lost
You're my libertine, a heart without a cause

Oh, oh what a joke
Wasted you'd laugh at the wrath of gods
Oh no, oh no
And feel it through the red in your eyes

Oh I found you with a Stella Artois
Empty and far, far gone
Many miles apart and lost
You're my libertine, our love without a cause

And my time is ticking, dividing pretty little things
To count them one by one
To kiss the Blarney Stone, it's already shown
That your mouth is a loaded gun

*To be heroic is to be courageous enough to die for
something; to be inspirational is to be crazy enough to live
a little.*

Metal

At last your million faces have driven me crazy
Oh baby won't you switch them daily
Yes it's crooked ink on the paper
And our calligraphy of hatred
'Cause we know you hate me
And now I'm fading as a product, a creation over time
Where love-made androids learn to lie

And in the coding rests a symbol
The lovely little metal
There's a tracker
Darling from hellish levels

And in the coding rests a symbol
The lovely little metal
There's a master
Darling of devilish bibles

Alas the way you made it when you called me baby
You only made me think of the way we used to say we
Were the haven of each other's safety
What made you different
What changed your wishes

And in the coding rests a symbol
The lovely little metal
There's a tracker
Darling from hellish levels

And in the coding rests a symbol
The lovely little metal
There's a master
Darling of devilish bibles

Like a spark from the twist of my wrists
Like a virus in the kiss of your lips

The blasphemy to be nothing but friends
That's the way it ends
The way it ends

Bad luck with women is a determined man's road to success. For every affliction, he makes, out of indignation, yet another advancement in order to exceed the man that the woman chose over him. This goes to show that great men are made great because they once learned how to fight the feeling of rejection.

Film Noir (Trade Some Resistance)

What's an un-lively moment when you're boldly writing history
I'd read a story to you but you're slowly fighting misery
And in fear of the future of this literary trickery

I only hated that you waited so long to introduce you to me
It reminds me of the time I waited for nothing, you see
It's not a gory allegory
Or even stealing from the rich and doing it poorly

It's simple darling, we make our own story

So let's go, let's go
It's made up darling played up
In our imaginations, trade some
Resistance for the fairytale kisses

My dear and you sir
You're my fiction literature
So we cross worlds, just a film noir for boys and girls
And every picture
Love is the reaper that steals our pearls

But I only hated that you waited so long to introduce you to me
It reminds me of the time I dated a mystery, you see

It's written already, and no secret they'll read it gladly

So let's go, let's go
It's made up darling played up
In our imaginations, trade some
Resistance for our fairytale kisses

Made up darling played up
In our imaginations, trade some
Resistance like they're fairytale kisses

Pride and power fall when the person falls, but discoveries of truth form legacies that can be built upon for generations.

Slipshod Lover

I took you 'round a carousel the size of Edinburgh
From the depths
Of a playful dark
I'm not a rebel don't care whether emotion is first
Like the best
Is the painful part

We know the thinkers of the morning
The night and the evening
What they think of us isn't the air we're breathing
So pardon my fierce
As I mark the list
For the scarred and muted, departed and losing side of the lovers'
super-sized ride

Oh I see
Yes I know you want me too
But I'm a dare
A little too dangerous for you
So feel the thrill
As I slowly pull the wild side out of you

Yes I know you want me too
The way you stare
A little too dangerous for you
Oh feel the thrill
As I slowly pull the wild side out of you

We forgot to look oh fell through the surface
Though minus the furnace the heart is still burning
So we start our clock
Tower and watch
Over the ocean-size and demonized, troubling frozen lake of fire

Oh I see
Yes I know you want me too

But I'm a dare
A little too dangerous for you
So feel the thrill
As I slowly pull the wild side out of you

Yes I know you want me too
The way you stare
A little too dangerous for you
Oh feel the thrill
As I slowly pull the wild side out of you

With a hint of good judgment, to fear nothing, not failure or suffering or even death, indicates that you value life the most. You live to the extreme; you push limits; you spend your time building legacies. Those do not die.

The Order Of Mistakes

If you show me that I'm a show-off
Take the glory from this know-it-all
Maybe I'll listen or do more
Baby I'd kiss you for
The first time
The first time
Won't you shoot a bird to fly

You stand taller than me but it's not even physically
Yeah the irony of it all
It's to never really speak but to manage to maul
So that night
As the body of Christ, yes you called me the frown of God
And then I called you mine in a massive brawl

Whether it's true or not
Or just a cute little smile
I kinda like you a lot
The way you love me
Way you love me up

Yeah she locks me, she locks me not

I kicked through glass to impress you with wrath
And you laughed at the shape of the crack
Do we win or do we lose
I'm no man, can't find his answer in booze
But at least you understand
Honey you comprehend without the burden of proof

Whether it's true or not
Or just a cute little smile
I kinda like you a lot
The way you love me
Way you love me up

Yeah she locks me, she locks me not

And I promise the mistakes are there to remember
'Cause order's the way I'd forever forget her
I promise, mistakes are there to remember
'Cause order's the way I'd forever forget her

Everyone judges constantly: positively judging one person is the same as negatively judging everyone else; it is to say that that person is superior in some sense.

Pressure Of The Hellhounds

To label is to negate me
And when I'm unstable
You're wide awake to a daydream

Where you think I wrestled an angel
I didn't sense the danger
At first, have you heard
You saw it coming
And thought it lovely
It's when you witness the anger
God's pain for the last girl
You hurt, and it works

What's the other way my lady
To drown me in glue
And wrap me in tape

Yes you're safe when the mind runs away
'Til the pressure of the hellhounds come your way
But you're

Strong enough to give your all
Baby strong enough to give it all
With a smirk on the face
And the kings at your waist
With a smirk on the face
And the kings at your waist

A lesson's only learned
When there's a scar to remind
It's zero history
But not hard to find
You share it and wear it
It howls, you hear it
But before it happens
Oh how'll you hear it

So we lost the way my lady
To drown me in glue
And wrap me in tape

Yes you're safe when the mind runs away
'Til the pressure of the hellhounds come your way
But you're

Strong enough to give your all
Baby strong enough to give it all
With a smirk on the face
And the kings at your waist
With a smirk on the face
And the kings at your waist

Yes you're safe when the mind runs away
'Til the pressure of the hellhounds come your way
But you're strong enough to give your all
Yes you're strong enough to give it all

Showing a lack of self-control is in the same vein granting authority to others: "Perhaps I need someone else to control me."

My Marionette

There are prophecies of fortune
Only suffering and torture
When it's never what you want
But you'd be in my head
To know what it meant when I said
"Your heart is all I want"

I'll send all I have
Right or wrong
It's poison it's edible
It won't be long

You struck the matches
You lit the fire
It rises higher, you're a marionette
You sharpened the razor
To cut off my fingers
You were my puppet, my marionette

There are rules to score
To win the hearts and lose more
The friendship's just a war
When envy stares through dark corridors
The gorgeous was the deadly
The rugged angel the medley

I'll send all I have
Right or wrong
'Cause they're both credible
It won't be long

You struck the matches
You lit the fire
It rises higher, you're a marionette
You sharpened the razor

To cut off my fingers
You were my puppet, my marionette

Love is as simple as the absence of self given to another. God, when invited, fills the void of any unrequited love; hence loving is how one is drawn closer to God no matter its most horrific repercussions.

Haze

I open the gates pay the fines of fate
Take a sip of tea 'til my knees grow weak
(I can't see)
By a spotlight twisting blinds
Plays the requiem of me
(New melodies)
Now shines the battle cry in our eyes
I'm a living sacrifice reversed we come alive

Every line every trace
Oh the eyes on the face
Where's the need for grace
Off my knees then I pace
To think unclear things
Like the fierce of hate
That was made and laid at the end of your parade
To follow as some pay for the fines of fate

So we're holding on to love
We're holding on like it's not okay
'Til promised a new day
We're holding on to love
We're holding on and love will stay
'Til there's a new way

We're blind in a lovely haze

I hold my breath for the rest let the surface rise
As the rest of the journey turns in our eyes
(Took a dive)
Scorching blood in a raging fire
Pouring shivers in a lazy spine
(Shocked to life)
We knife at fantasies and the heresy
The way of God was at odds with the things in me

Every line every trace
Oh the eyes on the face
Where's the need for grace
Off my knees then I pace
To think unclear things
Like the fierce of hate
That was made and laid at the end of your parade
To follow as some pay for the fines of fate

So we're holding on to love
We're holding on and love is stained
'Til promised a new day
We're holding on to love
We're holding on and love will stay
'Til there's a new way

We're blind in a lovely haze

We're holding on it's not okay
It's gonna stay
We're holding on and love is stained
It's gonna stay

We're blind in a lovely haze

Find a purpose to serve, not a lifestyle to live.

Münchausen

Showing your portrait of me
It's a joke that's unfortunately
Something I wasn't and wasn't meant to be

We pretend an answer
Even when it's right
The intent is the cancer
It's not the insight
A longing that we know not what
Sehnsucht
With equal force
Like we war by the gun

'Cause love is boring when it's not on the run

Münchausen what a syndrome
To get a kiss in the center of the room
Oh yes I know you
Though I join you
It's the festival of fools
And you carve me open with the metal tools

No need to see how it goes
The beginning's like the end
Oh you'd find coke in the snow
Just to start an argument
And you won't let it go
Every time
Every crime
Marks a monument oh, oh
A longing that we know not what
Sehnsucht
With equal force
Like we war by the gun

With no remorse like we're drunk in the sun

Münchausen what a syndrome
To get a kiss in the center of the room
Oh yes I know you
Though I join you
It's the festival of fools
And you starve me always oh yes it's true

To hear my own name is nothing but pain
You know how the blood'll flow
'Cause hypocrisy's the ladder to fame
As the honesty'll watch it grow
A longing that we know not what
Sehnsucht
With equal force
Like we war by the gun

Scarification, the skin is coarse and the innocence gone

Münchausen what a syndrome
To get a kiss in the center of the room
Oh yes I know you
Though I join you
It's the festival of fools
Where you carve me open with the metal tools

When a poet digs himself into a hole, he doesn't climb out. He digs deeper, enjoys the scenery, and comes out the other side enlightened.

Fable

By night you're a beautiful mistake
And pathetic to their naked eyes
A risk to take baby sacrifice to make
Still recovering and the medics were lies

So the innocent have paid in a world of hate
In the out-there way we've made

And now you're the tomb who rocks the cradle too
'Cause you're raw to the core
In love's womb it's still a fable to you
It's your peace through war

They'd fuel your doubt at any cost
And rust the heart, it's torn
And when you loved the things you lost
It was a drug to the mouth of scorn

You're the tomb who rocks the cradle too
'Cause you're raw to the core
In love's womb it's still a fable to you
It's a peace through war

There were 70 seats and you washed their feet
Will it be enough is it able
Oh love can be enough or the fable
Love can be enough or the fable

In the land where excellence is commended, not envied,
where weakness is aided, not mocked, there is no question
as to how its inhabitants are all superhuman.

Countdown To Kill Me

I open, I open
To a lithium flame
At my feet
I tried, I tried
To mirror lies
In my sleep
I'll never know, never ever know
Sensations of your prey
A dreamer's satellite breaks in the night of day

Three
It's not me
Two
Not me
One
Ever me
Zero
Suffering
Countdown to kill me

You know it, you know it
The darkness
On a poet
You tried, you tried
To stitch the eyes
Like a stoic
I'll never know, never ever know
Sensations of your prey
A dreamer's satellite breaks in the night of day

Three
It's not me
Two
Not me
One
Ever me

Zero
Suffering
Countdown to kill me

Seductively trash the game
And strike me in my sleep
In bitter sweetness untamed
Countdown from

Three
It's not me
Two
Not me
One
Ever me
Zero
Suffering
Countdown to kill me
Your countdown to kill me

"The tyrant dies and his rule is over; the martyr dies and his rule begins." ~Søren Kierkegaard

Lovecraft Theme

I'm self-proclaimed and left to find
Motivate darling won't you cross my mind
We've been here far too long
Electropathic crawling along
Horror's wings here the siren there
But taken as it seems
Endure oh yeah
Endure oh yeah
Endure stripes through Venerean air

You dream, we dream
Psychopathic dreams shout it out
And when the chips are down
It won't fade, it won't fade out

On every page you put your heart in it
In our Lovecraft theme
And every nightlight starts to darken
In our Lovecraft theme

There are leaps of faith
There are knights of faith
There are kings of faith
You're the reasoned faith
The strength in my own absurd

You dream, we dream
Psychopathic dreams shout it out
And when the chips are down
It won't fade, it won't fade out

On every page you put your heart in it
In our Lovecraft theme
And every nightlight starts to darken
In our Lovecraft theme

"A perfect faith would lift us absolutely above fear."
~George MacDonald

Wahrheit For My Sycophant (My Psychopath)

Take a step at a time
Take a step into time
Wanderer, it is written
Or call it crime after crime

Gain what's lost
Just to feel it's gone

Wahrheit for my sycophant
To hear it deaf and speak dumb
Wahrheit it's alright and it's
It's arsenic to my tongue

Oh the fear the phobia of the best
Baby guilt tattooed on the chest
We cross our fingers
But only some hope to die
The gorgeous way
The kind you come alive

Wahrheit for a sycophant
To hear it deaf and speak dumb
Wahrheit it's alright and it's
It's arsenic to the tongue
Wahrheit, my psychopath
To hear it deaf and speak dumb
Wahrheit it's alright and it's
It's arsenic to my tongue

You hear a voice
By nature you'd run
It's not really your choice
It came it's long gone
It says, it says

A fruitless year, take a fearless heart

One that blooms late will flourish in the dark

A fruitless year, take a fearless heart
One that blooms late will flourish in the dark
Oh the licking flames of our burning hearts
The fumes of this burning heart
You put the fierce in this burning heart

"I would rather a thousand times be a free soul in jail than to be a sycophant and coward in the streets." ~Eugene V. Debs

Shatter Me Sinfonia

Under pressure will you fly for me
Can you fly
Can you fly
Wing-length measured
A Fieseler under pressure

Anger's like an acid
Remember the last thing said
Will it explode the veins, erode the chains
Her road won't change it's hope through the rain
No she's not afraid, sweetness enraged and you know
You know love is insane
Neuro-pro at the game
Oh look at her game

Was it compassion for the hopeless the dust
Are they trashing her to be holy but not

Sinfonia, Sinfonia
To the music, frozen lake you'll open
Sin's lovelier, sin's lovelier
Under pressure, will the wings open
Sinfonia

Laid at the horse's heel to be laughed at in fear
Tossed on thin ice it's fuel for flight
I don't know why but it's the reason she prays
The season to try
It's treason we make 'cause a Caesar will die

Was it compassion for the hopeless the dust
Are they trashing her to be holy but not

Sinfonia, Sinfonia
To the music, frozen lake you'll open
Sin's lovelier, sin's lovelier

Under pressure, will the wings open
Sinfonia

Shatter me, oh the sight of your strength
Shatter me, oh your hidden white wings
Shatter me, shatter me

"Where words fail, music speaks." ~Hans Christian Andersen

Center Of War

Did we run from the world
Where sold out souls are laid out for sale
And devils reap chaos on a run from Hell
Where harmony has gone pale

(I see you glow in the spotlight of suns
Prophesying it's only begun)

Emotions bleed where love frowns and despair smiles
My home is within the core
In the center of this place lies my heart for love
My love is the center of war

Clairvoyance then something took flight
The prophecy of a proximity mine
I crave your love like it rises higher
Than the formula of the gods forming fire

(The dreams flow at the night light of the moon
Prophesying a wellness immune)

Emotions bleed where love frowns and despair smiles
My home is within the core
The center of this place lies, 'cause my heart's for love
My love is the center of war

(Doves flee the graveyard and no peace, save me Lord)

Emotions bleed where love frowns and despair smiles
My home is within the core
The center of this place lays my heart for love
My love is the center of war

"The true soldier fights not because he hates what is in front of him, but because he loves what is behind him."
~G.K. Chesterton

Jump The Gun

I have frostbite as you light Fortunas with the sun
You've outdone me
You've outdone me
Chess of Czeslaw
'Cause I jump the gun

And you don't wanna rip me apart
Don't wanna soak me in jet fuel light the card you are
My matinee of glory the only one
But I jump the gun
The philoverity of suffering
The philosophy to hate nothing

Frostbite as you light Fortunas with the sun
You've outdone me
You've outdone me
Chess of Czeslaw
'Cause I jump the gun

In a platonic love that grows more
And tomorrow Eros erotica by the shore
Love's evolution
The only revolution
Love's evolution
The hope for revolution

And you don't want the safety on
Don't want the safety that tunes out the fun we are
Bodies paralyzed minds buried alive
In a room soundproof
Fallen short of the gory abroad
Let's go beyond the facade

Frostbite as you light Fortunas with the sun
You've outdone me
You've outdone me

Chess of Czeslaw
'Cause I jump the gun

In a platonic love that grows more
And tomorrow Eros erotica by the shore
Love's evolution
The only revolution
Love's evolution
The hope for revolution

A platonic love that grows more
And tomorrow Eros erotica by the shore
A platonic love that grows more
And tomorrow Eros erotica by the shore

"I have leaned too much on the idea of being able to write
poetry, and if this is a frost I shall be rather stranded."
~C.S. Lewis

For Veritas Aequitas

You are, is what I know
So tell me to turn the helm
So tell me to pull the reins

You speak the mother tongue but it weighs a lot faster
And the waves are a ton oh your name is Vernacular
Selective fire you select your fire

Is it sin I wanna know
Should I call you mine
Or should I walk the line

I wanna know I wanna know
Should I call you mine
Or should I walk the line

And I hit the rock bottom 'cause I'm power hungry
And a man of doom
And the tastes of flames are so tasty for you
Power hungry's a man of doom
And the tastes of flames are so tasty for you

Should we take the reins but I'd hope for teenage love
It's unsure and untamed bloody wars and tugs
Await the Night Riviera wishing blind is love

Is it sane I wanna know
Should I call you mine
Or should I walk the line

I wanna know I wanna know
Should I call you mine
Or should I walk the line

For veritas aequitas
Fate will come and see us

Saying "love, it will find you"
It will find you

For veritas aequitas
Fate will come and see us
Showing love, it will find you
It will find you

Sometimes it takes a lowly, title-less man to humble the world. Kings, rulers, CEOs, judges, doctors, pastors, they are already expected to be greater and wiser.

Like St. Raphael

This is the upper class of madness
Where everything but something is lacking
The kind where love is about passing
Darling mastering an affection
It's the mother of mathematics
And to suffer is the lesson

Oh you know
I'm not a lover of tactics
Oh to throw
It all or nothing
It either flows in my blood or it doesn't happen

'Cause I feel like St. Raphael
For you I'd go through Hell
The price, the deal
Like a curse to heal
'Cause I'm your Raphael
I'm your Raphael

If I knew what to do
I'd do more than write a song for you
I have imperfections but a map with 3 directions
Yes it's Heaven
The dark and the last one is your heart
So I'm under pressure and on track
Baby nothing can tear me apart

'Cause I feel like St. Raphael
For you I'd go through Hell
The price, the deal
Like a curse to heal
'Cause I'm your Raphael
I'm your Raphael

Love is without a doubt the laziest theory for the meaning of life, but when it actually comes a time to do it we find just enough energy to over-complicate life again. Any devil can love, whom he himself sees as, a good person who has treated him well, but to love also the polar opposite is what separates love from fickle emotions.

Christopher James Gilbert (born May 29, 1987), better known by his pseudonym Criss Jami and by his alter ego TheKillosopher, is an American poet, essayist, existentialist philosopher, singer/songwriter, and the creator/designer of *Killosopher Apparel*.

His other works include:
-Salomé: In Every Inch In Every Mile (2011, author)
-Yesterday and Tomorrow (2011, co-author)

Printed in Great Britain
by Amazon

23522559R00037